Vehicle Maintenance

Log Book

Table of Contents

Vehicle Identification Card

Vehicle:		
Year:	Make:	Model:

Engine:

Vehicle Identification Number (VIN):

Purchase Date:

Mileage at Purchase:

Warranty / Additional Information:

Emergency Contact

Name	Address	Phone	Notes

Contact List

Name	Address	Phone	Notes

Insurance Information

Policy Number	Company	Effective Date	Expiration Date	Agent / Phone

Insurance Information

Policy Number	Company	Effective Date	Expiration Date	Agent / Phone

Monthly Checklist

Year:	Jan	Feb	Mar	Apr	May	Jun	Jul	Aug	Sep	Oct	Nov	Dec
Engine oil level												
Windshield washer fluid												
Coolant												
Brake fluid level												
Transmission fluid												
Power steering fluid												
Tire pressures												
Lights check												
Wipers / Windshield												
Interior and exterior cleanliness												

Monthly Checklist

Year:	Jan	Feb	Mar	Apr	May	Jun	Jul	Aug	Sep	Oct	Nov	Dec
Engine oil level												
Windshield washer fluid												
Coolant												
Brake fluid level												
Transmission fluid												
Power steering fluid												
Tire pressures												
Lights check												
Wipers / Windshield												
Interior and exterior cleanliness												

Monthly Checklist

Year:	Jan	Feb	Mar	Apr	May	Jun	Jul	Aug	Sep	Oct	Nov	Dec
Engine oil level												
Windshield washer fluid												
Coolant												
Brake fluid level												
Transmission fluid												
Power steering fluid												
Tire pressures												
Lights check												
Wipers / Windshield												
Interior and exterior cleanliness												

Monthly Checklist

Year:	Jan	Feb	Mar	Apr	May	Jun	Jul	Aug	Sep	Oct	Nov	Dec
Engine oil level												
Windshield washer fluid												
Coolant												
Brake fluid level												
Transmission fluid												
Power steering fluid												
Tire pressures												
Lights check												
Wipers / Windshield												
Interior and exterior cleanliness												

Monthly Checklist

Year:	Jan	Feb	Mar	Apr	May	Jun	Jul	Aug	Sep	Oct	Nov	Dec
Engine oil level												
Windshield washer fluid												
Coolant												
Brake fluid level												
Transmission fluid												
Power steering fluid												
Tire pressures												
Lights check												
Wipers / Windshield												
Interior and exterior cleanliness												

Monthly Checklist

Year:	Jan	Feb	Mar	Apr	May	Jun	Jul	Aug	Sep	Oct	Nov	Dec
Engine oil level												
Windshield washer fluid												
Coolant												
Brake fluid level												
Transmission fluid												
Power steering fluid												
Tire pressures												
Lights check												
Wipers / Windshield												
Interior and exterior cleanliness												

Monthly Checklist

Year:	Jan	Feb	Mar	Apr	May	Jun	Jul	Aug	Sep	Oct	Nov	Dec
Engine oil level												
Windshield washer fluid												
Coolant												
Brake fluid level												
Transmission fluid												
Power steering fluid												
Tire pressures												
Lights check												
Wipers / Windshield												
Interior and exterior cleanliness												

Monthly Checklist

Year:	Jan	Feb	Mar	Apr	May	Jun	Jul	Aug	Sep	Oct	Nov	Dec
Engine oil level												
Windshield washer fluid												
Coolant												
Brake fluid level												
Transmission fluid												
Power steering fluid												
Tire pressures												
Lights check												
Wipers / Windshield												
Interior and exterior cleanliness												

Monthly Checklist

Year:	Jan	Feb	Mar	Apr	May	Jun	Jul	Aug	Sep	Oct	Nov	Dec
Engine oil level												
Windshield washer fluid												
Coolant												
Brake fluid level												
Transmission fluid												
Power steering fluid												
Tire pressures												
Lights check												
Wipers / Windshield												
Interior and exterior cleanliness												

Monthly Checklist

Year:	Jan	Feb	Mar	Apr	May	Jun	Jul	Aug	Sep	Oct	Nov	Dec
Engine oil level												
Windshield washer fluid												
Coolant												
Brake fluid level												
Transmission fluid												
Power steering fluid												
Tire pressures												
Lights check												
Wipers / Windshield												
Interior and exterior cleanliness												

Oil Change Log

Date	Mileage	Description	Performed by / Company	Cost

Oil Change Log

Date	Mileage	Description	Performed by / Company	Cost

Oil Change Log

Date	Mileage	Description	Performed by / Company	Cost

Oil Change Log

Date	Mileage	Description	Performed by / Company	Cost

Oil Change Log

Date	Mileage	Description	Performed by / Company	Cost

Oil Change Log

Date	Mileage	Description	Performed by / Company	Cost

Maintenance / Repair / Service Log

Date	Mileage	Description	Performed by / Company	Cost	Notes / Warranty

Maintenance / Repair / Service Log

Date	Mileage	Description	Performed by / Company	Cost	Notes / Warranty

Maintenance / Repair / Service Log

Date	Mileage	Description	Performed by / Company	Cost	Notes / Warranty

Maintenance / Repair / Service Log

Date	Mileage	Description	Performed by / Company	Cost	Notes / Warranty

Maintenance / Repair / Service Log

Date	Mileage	Description	Performed by / Company	Cost	Notes / Warranty

Maintenance / Repair / Service Log

Date	Mileage	Description	Performed by / Company	Cost	Notes / Warranty

Maintenance / Repair / Service Log

Date	Mileage	Description	Performed by / Company	Cost	Notes / Warranty

Maintenance / Repair / Service Log

Date	Mileage	Description	Performed by / Company	Cost	Notes / Warranty

Maintenance / Repair / Service Log

Date	Mileage	Description	Performed by / Company	Cost	Notes / Warranty

Maintenance / Repair / Service Log

Date	Mileage	Description	Performed by / Company	Cost	Notes / Warranty

Maintenance / Repair / Service Log

Date	Mileage	Description	Performed by / Company	Cost	Notes / Warranty

Maintenance / Repair / Service Log

Date	Mileage	Description	Performed by / Company	Cost	Notes / Warranty

Maintenance / Repair / Service Log

Date	Mileage	Description	Performed by / Company	Cost	Notes / Warranty

Maintenance / Repair / Service Log

Date	Mileage	Description	Performed by / Company	Cost	Notes / Warranty

Maintenance / Repair / Service Log

Date	Mileage	Description	Performed by / Company	Cost	Notes / Warranty

Maintenance / Repair / Service Log

Date	Mileage	Description	Performed by / Company	Cost	Notes / Warranty

Maintenance / Repair / Service Log

Date	Mileage	Description	Performed by / Company	Cost	Notes / Warranty

Maintenance / Repair / Service Log

Date	Mileage	Description	Performed by / Company	Cost	Notes / Warranty

Maintenance / Repair / Service Log

Date	Mileage	Description	Performed by / Company	Cost	Notes / Warranty

Maintenance / Repair / Service Log

Date	Mileage	Description	Performed by / Company	Cost	Notes / Warranty

Maintenance / Repair / Service Log

Date	Mileage	Description	Performed by / Company	Cost	Notes / Warranty

Maintenance / Repair / Service Log

Date	Mileage	Description	Performed by / Company	Cost	Notes / Warranty

Date	Mileage	Description	Performed by / Company	Cost	Notes / Warranty

Maintenance / Repair / Service Log

Date	Mileage	Description	Performed by / Company	Cost	Notes / Warranty

Maintenance / Repair / Service Log

Date	Mileage	Description	Performed by / Company	Cost	Notes / Warranty

Maintenance / Repair / Service Log

Date	Mileage	Description	Performed by / Company	Cost	Notes / Warranty

Maintenance / Repair / Service Log

Date	Mileage	Description	Performed by / Company	Cost	Notes / Warranty

Maintenance / Repair / Service Log

Date	Mileage	Description	Performed by / Company	Cost	Notes / Warranty

Maintenance / Repair / Service Log

Date	Mileage	Description	Performed by / Company	Cost	Notes / Warranty

Maintenance / Repair / Service Log

Date	Mileage	Description	Performed by / Company	Cost	Notes / Warranty

Maintenance / Repair / Service Log

Date	Mileage	Description	Performed by / Company	Cost	Notes / Warranty

Maintenance / Repair / Service Log

Date	Mileage	Description	Performed by / Company	Cost	Notes / Warranty

Maintenance / Repair / Service Log

Date	Mileage	Description	Performed by / Company	Cost	Notes / Warranty

Maintenance / Repair / Service Log

Date	Mileage	Description	Performed by / Company	Cost	Notes / Warranty

Maintenance / Repair / Service Log

Date	Mileage	Description	Performed by / Company	Cost	Notes / Warranty

Maintenance / Repair / Service Log

Date	Mileage	Description	Performed by / Company	Cost	Notes / Warranty

Maintenance / Repair / Service Log

Date	Mileage	Description	Performed by / Company	Cost	Notes / Warranty

Maintenance / Repair / Service Log

Date	Mileage	Description	Performed by / Company	Cost	Notes / Warranty

Maintenance / Repair / Service Log

Date	Mileage	Description	Performed by / Company	Cost	Notes / Warranty

Maintenance / Repair / Service Log

Date	Mileage	Description	Performed by / Company	Cost	Notes / Warranty

Maintenance / Repair / Service Log

Date	Mileage	Description	Performed by / Company	Cost	Notes / Warranty

Maintenance / Repair / Service Log

Date	Mileage	Description	Performed by / Company	Cost	Notes / Warranty

Maintenance / Repair / Service Log

Date	Mileage	Description	Performed by / Company	Cost	Notes / Warranty

Maintenance / Repair / Service Log

Date	Mileage	Description	Performed by / Company	Cost	Notes / Warranty

Maintenance / Repair / Service Log

Date	Mileage	Description	Performed by / Company	Cost	Notes / Warranty

Maintenance / Repair / Service Log

Date	Mileage	Description	Performed by / Company	Cost	Notes / Warranty

Maintenance / Repair / Service Log

Date	Mileage	Description	Performed by / Company	Cost	Notes / Warranty

Maintenance / Repair / Service Log

Date	Mileage	Description	Performed by / Company	Cost	Notes / Warranty

Maintenance / Repair / Service Log

Date	Mileage	Description	Performed by / Company	Cost	Notes / Warranty

Maintenance / Repair / Service Log

Date	Mileage	Description	Performed by / Company	Cost	Notes / Warranty

Maintenance / Repair / Service Log

Date	Mileage	Description	Performed by / Company	Cost	Notes / Warranty

Maintenance / Repair / Service Log

Date	Mileage	Description	Performed by / Company	Cost	Notes / Warranty

Maintenance / Repair / Service Log

Date	Mileage	Description	Performed by / Company	Cost	Notes / Warranty

Maintenance / Repair / Service Log

Date	Mileage	Description	Performed by / Company	Cost	Notes / Warranty

Maintenance / Repair / Service Log

Date	Mileage	Description	Performed by / Company	Cost	Notes / Warranty

Maintenance / Repair / Service Log

Date	Mileage	Description	Performed by / Company	Cost	Notes / Warranty

Maintenance / Repair / Service Log

Date	Mileage	Description	Performed by / Company	Cost	Notes / Warranty

Maintenance / Repair / Service Log

Date	Mileage	Description	Performed by / Company	Cost	Notes / Warranty

Maintenance / Repair / Service Log

Date	Mileage	Description	Performed by / Company	Cost	Notes / Warranty

Maintenance / Repair / Service Log

Date	Mileage	Description	Performed by / Company	Cost	Notes / Warranty

Maintenance / Repair / Service Log

Date	Mileage	Description	Performed by / Company	Cost	Notes / Warranty

Maintenance / Repair / Service Log

Date	Mileage	Description	Performed by / Company	Cost	Notes / Warranty

Maintenance / Repair / Service Log

Date	Mileage	Description	Performed by / Company	Cost	Notes / Warranty

Maintenance / Repair / Service Log

Date	Mileage	Description	Performed by / Company	Cost	Notes / Warranty

Maintenance / Repair / Service Log

Date	Mileage	Description	Performed by / Company	Cost	Notes / Warranty

Maintenance / Repair / Service Log

Date	Mileage	Description	Performed by / Company	Cost	Notes / Warranty

Maintenance / Repair / Service Log

Date	Mileage	Description	Performed by / Company	Cost	Notes / Warranty

Maintenance / Repair / Service Log

Date	Mileage	Description	Performed by / Company	Cost	Notes / Warranty

Important Parts Information

Item	Details (size, type, part number...)	Additional Information / Notes
Tires	Size: Lug nut size :	
Oil	Oil filter details: Oil drain plug size:	
Fuel Filter	Part Number: Suggested mileage between changes:	
Air Filter	Part number: Suggested mileage between changes:	
Spark Plug	Size: Suggested mileage between changes:	
Serpentine Belt	Part number: Suggested mileage between changes:	

Important Parts Information

Item	Details (size, type, part number...)	Additional Information / Notes

Important Parts Information

Item	Details (size, type, part number...)	Additional Information / Notes

Important Parts Information

Item	Details (size, type, part number...)	Additional Information / Notes

Important Parts Information

Item	Details (size, type, part number...)	Additional Information / Notes

Important Parts Information

Item	Details (size, type, part number...)	Additional Information / Notes

Preferred Brands

Engine oil:	Air filter:
Brake fluid:	Fuel filter:
Transmission fluid:	Oil filter:
Coolant:	Wiper blades:
Power steering fluid:	Washer fluid:
Battery:	Spark plugs:

Notes

Notes

Notes

Notes

Notes

Notes

Notes

Made in United States
Orlando, FL
07 September 2024